Our American Family™

I Am Japanese American

Vivian Emery

The Rosen Publishing Group's
PowerKids Press™
New York

Published in 1997 by The Rosen Publishing Group, Inc.
29 East 21st Street, New York, NY 10010

Published in 1997 by The Rosen Publishing Group, Inc.
29 East 21st Street, New York, NY 10010

Copyright © 1997 by The Rosen Publishing Group, Inc.

First Edition

Book Design: Erin McKenna

Photo Credits: Cover © John Terence Turner/FPG International Corp.; photo illustration © Icon Comm./FPG International Corp.; p. 4 © Michael Krasowitz/FPG International Corp.; p. 7 © David Wade/FPG International Corp.; p. 8 © Dick Luria/FPG International Corp.; p. 11 © Travelpix/FPG International Corp.; p. 12 © Jane Forman Cigard/MIDWESTOCK; p. 15 © Keystone View Co./FPG International Corp.; p. 16 © Jean Kugler/FPG International Corp.; p. 19 © Travelpix/FPG International Corp.; p. 20 © Jim Hays/MIDWESTOCK.

Emery, Vivian.
    I Am Japanese American / by Vivian Emery.
        p.   cm. — (Our American family)
    Includes index.
    Summary: A Japanese American girl talks briefly about aspects of her heritage, including food, clothing, and religion.
    ISBN 0-8239-5011-5
    1. Japanese Americans—Juvenile literature.   [1. Japanese Americans.]   I. Title. II. Series.
E184.J3S86 1997
1973'.04956—dc21   23961   96-5392
  Eme   CIP
                                                      AC

Manufactured in the United States of America

Contents

1 Akiko   5
2 Japan   6
3 Respect   9
4 Shinto   10
5 Ikebana and Bonsai   13
6 Theater   14
7 Kimonos   17
8 Hina Matsuri   18
9 Food   21
10 Sharing Two Cultures   22
   Glossary   23
   Index   24

Akiko

Hi! My name is Akiko. I'm seven years old, and I live in Washington, DC. My brothers and I are Japanese Americans. My mom and dad came to the United States from a Japanese city called **Osaka** (oh-SAH-kah). Even though we live in the United States, my parents don't want us to forget our **heritage** (HEHR-ih-tij). So my family follows many Japanese **traditions** (truh-DISH-unz).

◀ My family and I speak both Japanese and English.

Japan

Japan is part of the continent of Asia. It's a chain of four big islands and lots of little islands in the Pacific Ocean. The capital of Japan is **Tokyo** (TOH-kee-oh). Our government is a **democracy** (de-MOK-ruh-see). The traditional leader of the country is Emperor Akihito. The main language in Japan is Japanese, but many people speak English too. In Japan, we call our country **Nipon** (nee-PON).

Tokyo is one of the world's most modern cities. ▶

Respect

My grandmother still follows all the Japanese traditions she learned when she was a little girl. Whenever I see her, we bow to each other. Bowing is a sign of politeness or affection. To the Japanese, **respect** (re-SPEKT) is very important. We are always **considerate** (kon-SID-er-it) of others. Older people are given the most **honor** (ON-er) because they have lived long enough to learn a lot and are very wise. I always bow lower than Grandmother. This shows that I respect her.

◀ Japanese traditions are often passed down from grandparent to grandchild.

9

Shinto

Our religion is called Shinto. Shinto honors the importance of nature. We believe in spirits, called Kami, that are all around us—in flowers, trees, lakes, and everywhere else in nature. Sometimes we go to a temple called a **shrine** (SHRYN). When we get there, we take off our shoes at the door and wash our mouths and hands with water. By doing these things, we show respect for the Kami. Then we can go inside to pray.

Some people pray in the Heian shrine in the Japanese city of Kyoto. ▶

Ikebana and Bonsai

My mother honors the beauty of nature with **ikebana** (ik-eh-BON-uh), or flower arranging. Each flower has to be placed in a very exact way because in ikebana everything has a special meaning. For example, the tallest flower stands for heaven, and the lowest one stands for the earth.

My mom collects **bonsai trees** (BONZ-eye TREEZ) too. These look exactly like the trees outside—except they're small enough to hold in your hands! Bonsai trees also remind us of the beauty of nature.

◄ To keep bonsai trees tiny, they are planted in very small containers, and are trimmed regularly.

13

Theater

Both of my brothers are actors. Yoshi, the younger one, takes **Noh** (NO) classes. Noh plays are usually old stories about Japanese history. The actors cover their faces with masks, and sometimes they wear wigs.

Seiji is a **Kabuki** (kuh-BOO-kee) actor. He wears a lot of makeup when he's on stage. Even though he doesn't have a mask like Yoshi, I can't always recognize him. Kabuki plays are more modern than Noh plays. The Kabuki plays tell stories about life in Japanese towns and cities.

Both men and women wear lots of makeup ▶ and bright costumes in Kabuki plays.

Kimonos

For special occasions, I wear a **kimono** (kih-MOH-noh). Kimonos are long robes that are made of colorful cloth and have special patterns on them. For winter, I have a kimono with snowflakes on it. For spring I wear one decorated with cherry blossoms. Around my waist, I tie an **obi** (OH-bee), or sash. I usually wear sandals and white socks with my kimono.

◀ Young girls and women alike wear kimonos.

17

Hina Matsuri

My favorite Japanese holiday is Hina Matsuri, or the Doll's Festival. Hina Matsuri honors the little girls in a family. Every year, on March 3, I wake up and put on a kimono. My parents give me two new dolls, which I put on a shelf that my father made just for them. The dolls stand for the Japanese Emperor and his wife, the Empress. Later that day, my cousins come over with their dolls. We have our own party, with green tea and rice cakes.

Many Japanese holidays are celebrated with great festivals. ▶

Food

My favorite food is **tempura** (tem-POOR-uh). Tempura is a dish made from chicken, shrimp, or vegetables that have been fried. My mom serves tempura with sauce and white rice. Sometimes we eat **sushi** (SOO-shee), which is raw fish served with vinegar rice and seaweed. My favorite fish is tuna. The traditional way to eat Japanese food is by using two long wooden sticks called chopsticks. Eating with chopsticks is harder for me than using a fork, but it's more fun.

◀ Many Japanese dishes are as beautiful to look at as they are delicious to eat!

21

Sharing Two Cultures

Being Japanese American means sharing two **cultures** (KUL-cherz). I may wear T-shirts and jeans most of the time, but I also have beautiful kimonos. I love hot dogs, but I also love tempura. My parents have a Fourth of July party to celebrate America's independence. But I also have a smaller party to celebrate Hina Matsuri. When I'm with my grandmother, she tells me what it was like to live in Japan. She hopes I won't forget our traditions. I promise her that I never will.

Glossary

bonsai tree (BONZ-eye TREE) A miniature tree.

considerate (kon-SID-er-it) Thinking of someone else's feelings.

culture (KUL-cher) The customs, art, and religions of a group of people.

democracy (de-MOK-ruh-see) A type of government that is run by the people.

heritage (HEHR-ih-tij) Cultural traditions that are handed down from parent to child.

honor (ON-er) To show respect and admiration for someone.

ikebana (ik-eh-BON-uh) The Japanese art of flower arranging.

Kabuki (kuh-BOO-kee) A kind of Japanese drama.

kimono (kih-MOH-noh) A long, colorful robe.

Nipon (nee-PON) The Japanese name for Japan.

Noh (NO) A kind of Japanese drama.

obi (OH-bee) A sash or belt for a kimono.

Osaka (oh-SAH-kah) A city in Japan.

respect (re-SPEKT) Feeling strong admiration for someone.

shrine (SHRYN) A Japanese temple.

sushi (SOO-shee) A Japanese dish made from raw fish, rice, and seaweed.

tempura (tem-POOR-uh) A Japanese dish made from fried vegetables, shrimp, or chicken.

Tokyo (TOH-kee-oh) The capital of Japan.

tradition (truh-DISH-un) The customs and beliefs that are handed down from parent to child.

Index

A
Akihito, Emperor, 6

B
bonsai trees, 13
bowing, 9

C
culture, 22

H
heritage, 5
Hina Matsuri
    (Doll's Festival),
    18, 22
honor, 9

I
ikebana, 13

K
Kabuki, 14
Kami, 10
kimono, 17, 18,
    22

N
nature, 10, 13
Nipon, 6
Noh, 14

O
obi, 17
Osaka, 5

R
religion, 10
respect, 9, 10

S
Shinto, 10
shrine, 10
sushi, 21

T
tempura, 21
Tokyo, 6
traditions, 5, 9,
    22